BOOKWORMS

T0005268

Sometimes We Feel Afraid

By Caitie McAneney

Cavendish
Square

New York

Published in 2022 by Cavendish Square Publishing, LLC
243 5th Avenue, Suite 136, New York, NY 10016

Library of Congress Cataloging-in-Publication Data

Names: McAneney, Caitie, author.
Title: Sometimes we feel afraid / Caitie McAneney.
Description: New York : Cavendish Square Publishing, [2022] | Series: Dealing with your feelings | Includes index.
Identifiers: LCCN 2020030660 | ISBN 9781502659842 (library binding) | ISBN 9781502659828 (paperback) | ISBN 9781502659835 (set) | ISBN 9781502659859 (ebook)
Subjects: LCSH: Fear in children–Juvenile literature. | Fear–Juvenile literature.
Classification: LCC BF723.F4 M44 2022 | DDC 155.4/1246–dc23
LC record available at https://lccn.loc.gov/2020030660

Editor: Caitie McAneney
Designer: Deanna Paternostro

CPSIA compliance information: Batch #CS22CSQ: For further information contact Cavendish Square Publishing LLC, New York, New York, at 1-877-980-4450.

Printed in the United States of America

Find us on

CONTENTS

Feeling Afraid

Have you ever felt afraid? Being afraid means feeling fear. Everyone feels fear sometimes. It's **normal** to be scared of things. You don't have to feel **shame** for being afraid.

5

What are you afraid of?
You might be afraid of dogs.
You might be afraid of snakes.
You might be afraid of
the dark. You might be afraid
of flying on a plane.

Sometimes we worry about change. You might be afraid of moving to a new house. You might be afraid of leaving home to go on a trip. You might be afraid of starting a new grade at school.

Fear is important. It tells us when something might hurt us. A fear of sharks can keep you safe in the ocean. A fear of falling can make you more careful. You can use fear to stay safe.

Sometimes we feel fear even when we're safe. You might be afraid of singing in front of people. You might worry about messing up. You can find ways to deal with fear so it doesn't stop you.

What Does Fear Feel Like?

How does fear feel in your body? You might find it hard to breathe. Your face might get hot. Your **stomach** might hurt. Your heart might beat faster. You might even cry.

14

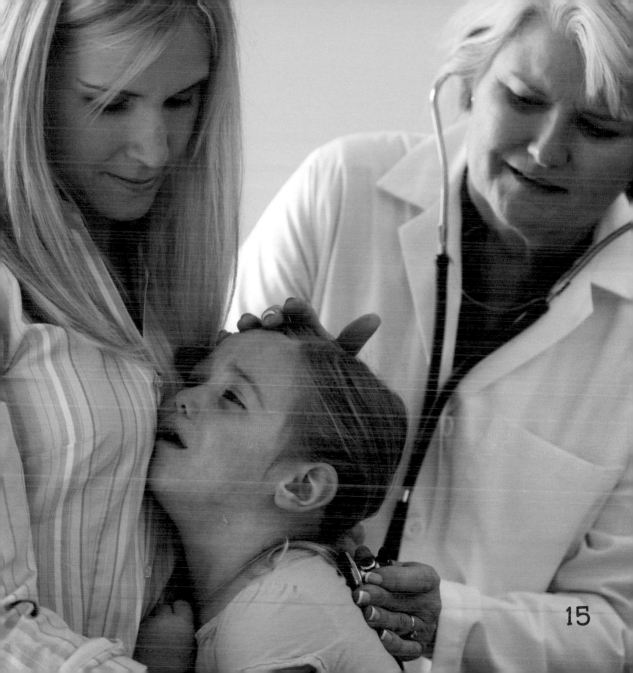

What does fear feel like in your mind? It might be hard to **focus**. You might feel on edge. You might think scary thoughts over and over. You might want to run away. You might stop in place.

Fear can take over your body and mind. It tells your body there is danger. It gets your body ready to fight, run away, or stop in place. These feelings will pass in a short time.

Fighting Fear

You can deal with your fears.
First, breathe in and out slowly.
Ask yourself why you are
afraid. Is there real danger?
If so, call for help or get to
safety. If not, just breathe.
The feeling will pass.

Feeling afraid doesn't have to hold you back from good, safe things. You can sing out loud. You can learn to swim. You can fly on a plane. Try new things. You are more than your fear!

23

WORDS TO KNOW

focus: To direct attention at something.

normal: Usual.

shame: Feeling like you are wrong or have done something wrong.

stomach: A body part that helps break down food.

INDEX

24